MW00880946

Maa Kheru

Thomas Renfrid
©2018

Contents

Copyright and Legal Notices

Maa Kheru

Actual Persons Disclaimer

This book is a work of fiction. Any resemblance of characters herein to real persons is purely coincidental.

Dedication

To anyone who has ever dreamed,
ever wondered,
ever pondered,
the why,
the where,
the how...

To anyone who has ever dreamed,
of worlds of wonder,
of worlds fantastical,
of worlds mythical,
of worlds,
steeped in the mystical...

To anyone who has ever dared,
to open the door,
to find the magic inside...

This book is for you...

Acknowledgements

I'd like to thank the author E.J. Wilson, who helped to proofread as well as give invaluable help in the departments of: formatting, style, and grammar, as well as guiding me through the publishing process. I'd also like to thank Zachry Wheeler, RJ Mirabal, Victor Aquista, and Daniel McDonald, whose encouragement gave me the confidence and inspiration to compile this collection and to follow my passion. I'd also like to thank the author and artist Erin Montgomery whose wonderful artwork will appear in the second edition of this collection.

I thank you all for the invaluable help, ideas, insights and encouragements on this journey.

Introduction

It was Edgar Allan Poe's classic tale of *The Raven,* with its wonderfully eerie atmosphere and poignant story telling; as well as Dr. Maya Angelou's strength of spirit found in poems such as *Still I Rise,* that helped inspire me to write in my own poetic style.

It was authors like J.R.R. Tolkien, C.S. Lewis, J.K. Rowling, Jim Butcher, and Kim Harrison... All of their works I absolutely adore and cherish, that helped inspire me to dream, to wonder, to ponder!

This collection explores the heart and soul of the ancient Egyptian gods and goddesses, going beyond the mythology to reveal the true essence that lies within...

This is just the beginning,
there are worlds unending,
just waiting to be explored...

So let us begin,
at the beginning of it all...

1. Amun: Infinite Heart

I

Timeless peace,
an infinity,
stillness,
in which,
all things begin,
from which,
all things spring...

Deep within,
the heart of Amun,
lies sleeping,
and within,
he lies dreaming,
and in dreaming,
is the beginning,
of all...

Endless possibility,
patterns shifting,
in colors uncountable,
and in joyous dance,
burst forth,
and in exquisite rush,

suffuse all...

Seeds of life,
universes born,
deep within,
the heart of Amun...

Seeds of life,
become,
spheres dancing,
spun round,
in ecstatic embrace,
for at the core,
lies Amun,
and within each,
is the infinite heart,
of all...

II

In the dreaming,
was born the duat...

The place of infinity,
of possibility,
of worlds,
of wonder,
of mind,
of matter,

of heart,
and soul...

In this vast,
and starry sea,
exist all things,
and all things,
are infinite,
eternal...

This infinity,
this eternity,
is the dream,
is the heart,
of Amun...

III

Within the heart,
lie jewels,
innumerable,
splendorous,
of colors unimaginable,
of beauty unspeakable...

Essence of joy,
essence of love,
endless potential,
held within,

the moment of creation....

Seeds of life,
scattered about,
in sacred array...

This starry sea,
this vast expanse,
is the essence,
of Amun...

IV

Dreaming star,
of sacred,
citrine fire,
in deepest dreams...

Dreaming deeply,
dreamt in tones,
of sapphire,
of aquamarine,
of emerald,
of carnelian...

Tones,
spinning,
spiraling,
merging...

And with sacred fire,
did emerge,
the sacred heart...

The Earth took form,
and from its blessed birth,
in sacred union,
man was born...

And within Earth,
and within man,
there abides,
the infinite heart,
of Amun...

V

In wonder,
with eyes anew,
man sees,
the skies alight...

Patterns of light,
shifting,
spinning round,
dancing,
in eternal rhythm...

And with ears anew,
he hears,
their song so pure...

Singing in a language,
transcendent,
singing,
of dreams spun,
of worlds begun,
singing,
the song of creation...

A sound so heavenly,
his heart is filled,
with love,
so deep,
his heart aches...

A sound,
that reverberates,
in every fiber,
of his being...

Calling,
uplifting,
singing,
saying...

Remember...

He weeps,
in joy so deep,
it aches,
in sorrow so deep,
he cries...

He reaches out...

In love,
the sound answers,
in surprise,
he cries,
in tenderness,
the sound enfolds him...

In love eternal,
he is blessed,
in love eternal,
he remembers,
in love eternal,
his eyes see...

In awe,
he holds in his arms,
a being,
he has never seen before,
such beauty,
beheld in the other's eyes...

Within his eyes,
worlds beheld,
within his eyes,
infinity,
within his eyes,
he sees himself,
reflected...

In the eyes of each other,
they see,
in the embrace of each other,
they remember,
and in the heart of each other,
they feel,
the song of creation,
the heart of creation...

They remember,
the infinite heart,
of Amun...

VI

In love,
they came,
in love,
they answered,
in love,

they searched,
in love,
they were,
with man...

In love,
they guided,
in love,
they taught,
in love,
they healed...

So in love,
was man,
that in yearning,
in searching,
they became,
gods...

So in love,
were they,
with man,
they forgot,
themselves...

So in love,
they forgot,
and became,
what they thought,

man needed...

So in love,
they became,
gods...

So in love,
they lost,
their hearts,
they lost,
their source...

The source,
from which,
all things spring,
in which,
all things,
are interwoven...

The infinite heart,
of Amun...

VII

In love,
He comes,
in love,
He reminds,
in love,

He embraces,
all...

He is,
the infinite heart,
He is,
in the hearts of all,
He is,
Amun...

2. Ra: The Essence of All

Golden rays,
like water,
flowing round,
shimmering,
encircling,
an essence...

An essence pure,
as diamond bright,
an essence,
of love...

Heart of love,
river of life,
entwined within...

Guide,
higher essence,
the soul of life,
the soul within,
us...

Centerpoint,
the balance,
held within...

Balance of mind,
balance of heart,
balance of soul,
held within...

It is the ka,
within all,
it is the light,
golden brilliance,
that shines,
steadfast,
It is Ra,
the soul,
the golden sun,
the essence,
of us all...

3. Sekhmet: Love's Essence

Blazing sun,
emerald fire,
blazing bright,
force of Love,
heart of Love...

Arrayed throughout,
shimmering in tones,
brightly beheld...

Within its center,
are we held,
standing upon,
Love's foundation,
enfolded,
we are filled,
with Love's presence...

Held within,
our highest sight,
our greatest being,
the state of grace,
is Love's blessing...

Joyous being,
so brightly lit,

alight in Love,
is Love's will...

Fire from within,
the spark is lit,
the flame of courage,
shining bright,
this is,
Love's essence...

Spark of life,
essence of life,
the flames of Love,
everywhere present,
in all things,
unending,
this is,
Love's strength...

Sekhmet,
star of Love,
shining brightly,
fiercely blazing,
beacon to all,
proclaiming,
love to all,
igniting,
love in all...

All this,
she is...

All this,
we are...

The essence of Love...

4. Osiris: Soul's Essence

Heavenly phoenix,
of sacred,
and starry flame,
in sapphire,
it shimmers...

Soaring,
it peacefully glides,
though twilight skies...

Whose passage,
in sonorous joy,
sweetly sings...

sings,
of the soul,
sings,
of transformation,
sings,
in lamentation...

In whose song,
is healing,
is remembering,
is rebirth...

17

In whose essence,
is eternity,
is love,
is Osiris...

It is the essence,
of us...

5. The Soul Of Isis

Two souls,
dance eternal,
ever entwined,
in love's embrace...

In love so deep,
as they gaze,
one upon the other,
forgotten,
is time...

As they gaze,
one into the other,
a universe
is found...

In love's fire,
it is born...

The heart of it,
aflame,
in love's desire...

With passions unbound,
in love profound,
two souls,

forever,
are one...

Within this sacred space,
lay dreams,
of boundless imagining,
in infinite possibility,
for in love,
are all things...

In love's union,
magick is born,
bespelling them,
in enchantment,
so wondrous...

Held captive,
in the arms,
of love,
drawn,
into its gravity,
inexorably,
becoming one...

They are transformed,
in love's alchemy,
each,
now a part,
of the other...

In love's fusion,
is found,
the seed,
of hope,
of wonder,
of life...

This is the essence,
of life,
of love...

It is the essence,
of Isis...

It is the essence,
of us...

6. Horus: Clarion Heart

Flying high,
soaring,
through honeyed sky,
gliding,
upon summer's
sweet breeze,
rides the falcon,
falling free...

Diving,
through skies,
of ambered blue,
with keenest eyes,
its prey is sighted,
circling,
it calls...

With the voice of the wind,
hauntingly,
it cries,
a sound so pure,
the heart,
cant help but weep,
in aching,
and ardent,
joy...

Hearing this,
a man looks,
up into the sky,
seeing,
the falcon,
so free,
he stands,
yearning,
and with hands raised,
he surrenders...

With eyes locked,
peering within,
the falcon's heart,
he sees,
the purity,
of his soul,
and in the fires,
of it's essence,
the form,
of his past,
is cast asunder...

Arisen,
held aloft,
in falcon's wings,
his heart is held,
reborn,

he remembers,
he is free...

He is,
the falcon,
Horus,
flying free...

7. Thoth: Awakened Be

I

The endless void,
forever stretching,
forever reaching,
in darkness,
enshrouded,
are its hands,
holding me...

End over end,
I tumble,
spinning,
slowly,
endlessly,
in its grasp...

Darkness,
all around,
I feel,
the unseen...

In distances unknowable,
immeasurable,
I hear,
their echoes,

25

calling,
in lamentation...

Remember...

All around,
their voices cry,
a keening wail,
louder,
insistent,
a wrenching sob,
so deep,
so terrible,
it fills me,
with dread sorrow...

It breaks my heart...

Louder still,
with fractured
and maddening sigh,
their voices beat,
upon my being,
like a howling wind...

A fever pitch,
so high,
until finally,
in tempest gale,

I am enveloped,
swept away...

II

Upon the raging winds,
my being is cast,
spun round,
broken down,
within cyclonic flux,
in quantum fermion,
I am sent beyond,
to the edge of reason...

Upon crystal shores I am cast,
in jarring realization,
I awaken,
in sudden light,
at once,
I am,
in blind awe...

In radiant pearlescence,
I am surrounded,
I look,
and am filled,
with its warm glow...

27

Before me,
the very land,
around me shifts,
turns,
twists...

Upon the air,
is heard,
a soft,
sonic resonance,
a sweet melody,
of orchestral majesty,
in a moment of bliss,
it soothes my soul...

Before me,
the light softens,
seems to withdraw,
and I feel,
a yearning ache,
so deep,
so keen,
so sharp,
that I cry,
crystal tears...

At once,
I am filled with love,
seeing before me,

the light condensed,
becoming a star,
so beautiful,
its splendor,
beyond compare,
its color,
all of them,
and beyond...

Before it,
I am seated,
deep within,
my heart resonates,
as one,
with this crystal sun...

Peering within,
patterns emerge,
spinning,
in shifting array,
the story begins...

III

Into its mesmerous mystery,
I am drawn,
down,
into its depths...

29

Below me,
a vast land,
lay sprawled,
in burgeoning beauty...

A land,
of spired towers,
of temples,
of cities,
all in colors,
of crystaled hue...

The people,
were of every shape,
every size,
every type,
of life,
that ever could be,
beyond imagining...

In the streets,
the children played,
in the temples,
the people prayed,
and in the schools,
were such wonders,
the children stayed,
absorbing all,
in utter glee...

In the halls of science,
all seekers sought,
the names,
the forms,
and the formulas,
of God...

Weaving such spells,
such alchemical,
and wonderful,
enchantments...

Enchanting the names of God,
calling His name,
in formulaic utterance...

"Quantus Majorana...
et lux sylicatum...
et artificium technologia...
et technologia omnipotens...
scientia est deus..."

They sought to understand,
to know His ways,
but in their wonder,
in their awe,
they forgot...

In their ignorance,
Pride came among them,
along with him,
he brought his brother,
Chaos,
and together,
they sought to control,
to bend,
to twist,
and to warp,
the very fabric,
of Nature herself,
and of all creation...

In fear the people ran,
cowering,
hiding,
from Chaos
yet wherever they went,
Pride surely did follow,
and before long,
Chaos found them...

Until there was nothing,
the very fabric,
of reality,
of existence,
was wrent asunder...

Screaming,
falling through,
the people pleaded...

"save us!
restore us!
free us!
from this evil dream!..."

Yet too long,
in the service,
of Chaos,
of Pride,
did they fall,
their calls unheeded...

For they forgot...

Until one among them,
did awaken,
and within him,
a light did begin,
to shine...

IV

searching for God,
I reached up,
searching...

All around,
explosion of wonder,
turning inside out,
looking,
reaching,
for God,
wanting to know...

In awe and wonder,
i look,
i take it in,
and,
am turned,
in and out,
a river,
my soul,
becomes,
turning,
in and out,
back,
on itself,
filled with the knowing,
of God,
filled with the love,
of God,
in vibrations ecstatic,
held,
suspended,

in a moment,
orgasmic,
my soul,
finally knows...

God is within...

V

I am free!,
we are free!,
from the nightmare,
if we remember...

Awakening from the dream,
I find myself,
sitting,
facing the star crystal,
but next to me,
is another,
a man,
not too dissimilar,
from me...

He smiles,
takes my hand,
and tells me,

"I bid you remember,

that you not repeat,
our mistakes...

I bid you peace,
and fare you well..."

Wait I say,
what be your name?
please clear my confusion...

To me he says,

"Many names have I,
and that I have done,
already...

But one among them,
is Thoth...

But it is also you,
for we are one...

Awaken..."

In wonder,
I do so,
with a start...

In awe,

I wonder...

Could it be?...

And my heart answers,

"YES!..."

And I marvel,
for there,
the answer be...

8. The Song of Amun

In the blink of Time,
held between the pause,
between Life's breath,
and Time's death,
stands the universe...

In softest tones,
spun of purest light,
arrayed in the hues,
of gossamer gold,
spun in silken white,
sparkling of the dust,
of Heart's delight,
spins the universe,
the universe within...

Held within,
the facets of life,
lay dear,
in orbit eternal,
spun round,
the heart,
so dear...

In this moment,
is the choice,

made bear...

The self aware,
between Maat and chaos,
standing betwixt...

Poised upon the abyss,
choices made,
whether to stand,
with Maat,
in the heart,
of all...

Or fall,
and into chaos,
disintegrate,
alone,
lost,
in dread,
forgotten...

Or so it seems...

For within the heart,
lies strength,
the spirit,
the heart of God,
in all...

Within all things,
is the resonance,
the sound,
the song,
of God,
the song of Amun...

This is the heart of Matter,
this is the heart of Maat,
its every molecule,
in exultant ecstasy,
its existence,
made vibrant,
by the voice of Amun...

Heed the call,
sing the song,
and fear is not...

For in joy,
chaos ceases,
in joy,
forgotten,
in joy,
remember...

We are one,
we are within,
the God-heart,

we are...

The song of Amun...

9. Shu: The Breath Of Life

In this infinite moment,
time stands still,
ceases,
is not...

Colors bright and vibrant,
seas of softest blue,
and jasmine green,
within the two,
bespeckled in jewel tones,
these flowers,
these stars,
sweetly calling,
their names,
their scents,
so softly carried,
on the air...

Its currents,
softly unseen,
carrying within it,
the echoes,
of times past,
of worlds beyond,
formed of the Love,
of the sun,

as it gently caresses,
and sweetly plays,
frolicking,
in our hair,
bringing with it,
the infusion of new life,
as it gently wraps us,
in its arms of light,
of Love...

The indrawn breath,
renewing,
the life within,
carrying the Love,
to each and every part,
and in the moment,
creating,
all things...

Its essence,
infinite,
the soul of creation...

Its essence,
the sun,
its molecules,
the ocean,
its breath,
life itself...

Its foundation,
the soul of being...

It is the beginning,
unending...

Worlds dance in its sway,
all the while singing its song,
of creation,
along the way...

It is God within,
coming alive,
and in the moment,
the soul,
the universe,
reborn...

The outblown breath,
the divine spark,
the river,
of hope,
of Love,
of life...

In its wake,
creation is,
the essence of Love...

Within the outbreath,
the softest surrender,
the sweetest sound,
of Shu,
and in sacred embrace,
God within,
opens His eyes,
He looks upon the world,
and smiles...

10. Tefnut: The Ocean of Love, of Life

Caressed by the twilit sky,
clad in the rainbow of dusk,
swelling seas,
shimmering in lavender,
streaked with purple,
gently roll,
a cosmic dance,
in rhythmic cadence,
set to the beat,
of Love's heart...

Nightly kissed,
by the moon,
bathed,
in its silvered,
evanescence,
its colors dance upon her skin,
in fond remembrance...

So softly,
the sweetest winds caress,
a gentle touch,
that holds within,
a longing,
and a Love,
fathoms deep,

of such unending,
enduring,
intensity...

Such longing,
fathoms deep,
in the ocean's heart,
ever upward,
it reaches,
for that infinite moment,
and in loving embrace,
holds the wind,
to her heart,
in eternity...

The sound of their union,
a thunderous roar,
that crashes upon the shore,
in wave after wave,
of endless Love...

And in their joining,
molecule upon molecule,
their bond eternal,
the chain of their Love,
ever unbroken...

From their bond,
in their Love,

life was born...

Lit from within,
the waters dance,
sparkling,
in bioluminous delight,
forming configurations,
the living ocean speaks...

Beckoning,
calling all,
to listen,
to see,
to hear,
life's ancient story...

Thus began,
this dance of Love,
born in sound,
and in silence,
Between breath,
and life,
a universe of Love,
is found,
is formed,
of the union,
of their hearts,
and their Love,
their essence,

is the foundation,
of all...

This is the story,
of Love,
of life,
their every molecule,
the basis of all...

Their story,
is our story,
is of you,
is of me,
is about everyone,
and the Love,
we've found...

Lover,
by any name,
I would know thee,
name you Tefnut,
or name me Shu,
still I would know you,
were you named You,
and I named Me,
still I would know thee,
for this is Love,
and so it must be,
here in the heart, of You and Me...

11. Nut & Geb: Love Eternal

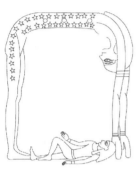

In the time of dreams,
in the between,
when twilit sky,
lay upon the ground,
duskly lit,
the arms of night,
enfold the land,
in the arms of love...

Upon the sand she dances,
turning,
gently swaying,
slowly spinning,
swirling,
with unseen grace...

Her very being,
the essence,
the pearlescence,
of amethyst azure,
she arrayed,
in the dust of stars,
weaving the dreams,
of a new day...

Under her spell,

the land awakens,
and arising,
before her stands,
a man,
alight,
ablaze,
in the glow,
of emerald gold,
his eyes,
two jewels,
of deepest jade,
his form,
amorphous,
as sand,
swirling,
gently shifting,
swaying,
in her trance...

Seeing her,
he surges forward,
his heart,
the light,
of love expanding...

Together,
they come,
eyes meeting,
within them,

worlds,
endless,
in infinite beginning,
in their touch,
the seed,
in their embrace,
love,
creation,
unending...

As one,
passionately,
they dance,
meeting,
merging,
their essence,
a whirlwind,
of love,
forged evermore...

Dancing together,
gazing,
eye to eye,
held within,
each other,
are worlds born,
and together,
are worlds spun,
woven,

throughout the land,
the essence,
the dance,
of their love,
eternal...

Born of their dreams,
is man,
he holding in turn,
the woman,
of his dreams,
dancing together,
in love,
their embrace,
the mirror,
of the other...

In their eyes,
an infinity,
of love,
is found...

In their hearts,
a love,
so deep,
so true,
exponential,
growing,
evermore...

Deep within,
their heart,
is found,
Love,
the source,
of all...

Each,
the mirror,
of the other,
and deep within,
the heart,
of All,
is Amun,
and we,
His heart,
His mirror,
His essence,
evermore...

12. Anubis: Healer Of Souls

I

As liquid amber,
the sun shines,
in the sky,
suspended,
its rays golden,
blossoming,
alighting,
upon flowers vermilion,
their petals delicate,
welcoming,
embracing the sun's,
honeyed nectar...

In tones jeweled,
of ruby,
and gold,
with wings,
of silvered,
and aqua blue,
the humming bird shimmers,
in stately dance,
it darts,
among the flowers,
in serenity,

55

it bows,
majestically,
to each in turn,
sipping sweetly,
inquiring of each,
the state of the day...

All at once,
and without warning,
the world,
weary of its weight,
slips,
freed,
from the grasp of time...

suspended,
frozen,
all is held,
immobile...

The last breath...

Light fades,
as above,
the sky,
once royal,
now is drawn,
in night's shade...

As above,
the sun,
a black star becomes,
in mourning shrouded,
its surface,
the sea of darkness,
in despair,
it shudders,
wreathed in the silver fire,
of its grief...

The gates of death,
once more,
are open...

Where once life abound,
now none is found...

Upon the ground,
lay heaped,
the dead,
decomposed,
their essence,
a spectral fog,
silver hued,
enshrouding all...

Their bones,
bleached,

scattershot,
throughout the land...

Dread despair,
mortal terror,
madness,
the anguish of loss,
these linger,
an echo in the air...

In storms cacophonous,
they rage,
in winds unceasing,
wailing,
keening,
a mournful cry,
raining,
in lost lament...

All seems hopeless...

II

In death,
we wonder,
shrouded,
in night's shade...

Each step,

walking,
upon the bones,
ancient,
gone to dust,
crushed,
their lives lost,
their stories,
spun in the wind,
their voices,
scattered,
in the sad,
bitter gale...

Lost in eternity,
we walk,
the only relief,
in this endless night,
the silver aura,
cast upon the land,
by the night's
dark sun...

Its pale glow,
only the faintest light,
illuminating,
the odd,
and mad specters,
that pass our way...

Endlessly,
we walk,
until a light,
so bright,
shines,
beckoning...

Faintly,
the embers kindle,
the fire of hope,
once lost,
again burns...

In the blink of an eye,
we find ourselves,
upon the shore,
of a great,
black river,
within which,
sits a ship,
gently swaying,
it seems to shimmer,
to shift,
shaping itself,
by the sailor's whim...

To some,
a barge of gold,
inlaid,

in onyx and jet,
to others,
decayed,
and with sails,
tattered,
and torn,
worn by age,
and element,
and still others,
in configurations strange,
and beyond all knowing...

Upon this ship we board,
to lands unknown,
but far better,
we hope,
than here...

Upon the deck,
there comes a figure,
grim and terrifying,
it is death itself,
enrobed in the grief,
of lifetimes past,
its very presence,
the essence of fear...

Embarking,
upon night's river,

we tremble in terror,
awaiting what judgment,
comes upon us...

All along the shore,
are scenes,
gruesome,
and macabre,
and at once,
haunting,
and sorrowful,
it is the resonance,
the memory,
of lives,
of people,
gone before...

Lost in fear,
slave to dread,
all around,
darkness pervades,
consuming,
our essence,
our sanity,
our soul...

On the edge of madness,
we are balanced,
falling into the void...

III

Awakened,
we are free,
the nightmare,
ceases to be...

Awakened,
I see,
a figure,
radiant,
with love,
it's robes arrayed,
in pastel hues,
of softest lavender blue,
it's essence,
the white-gold,
of a soft,
summer afternoon...

I stand before the doors,
of judgment,
of knowledge,
of self...

I enter,
and find not judge,
nor jury,

but a pool,
around which,
others wait,
in love,
they greet me,
and bid me look...

Before me,
my life is laid bare,
the good,
the bad,
the indifferent,
to learn and share...

They bid me enter,
and together,
Death and I,
submerge,
cleansed,
we arise,
one looking upon the other,
In awe,
I realize,
He is me,
and together,
we merge,
for we are one,
and together,
we are reborn...

our journey,
neverending...

I am you...
I am Anubis...

13. Nephthys: The Call of Home

With wonder,
I look upon,
the evanescent splendor,
that all around,
surrounds me...

In awe,
I wonder,
at the oceans,
of peace,
as they cascade,
pervading me,
so deeply,
in their ecstasy...

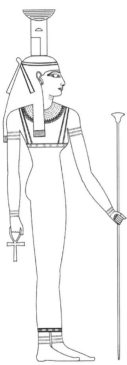

As deep within,
these waves call,
echoing,
the thrum,
the pulse,
the rhythm,
of my soul...

I surrender,
to the waves of Love,
and find within,

their opalescence,
the essence,
the sheen of truth...

In resonance,
they call,
awakening my soul...

Saying remember...

In vain it seems,
I wondered,
I sought,
I pondered,
I searched,
and studied...

In all the disciplines,
of the heavens,
and the earth,
I sought,
yearning,
to quench this fire,
that ever burns,
in my soul,
never sated,
this burning desire,
to know God,
to know myself,

to remember...

Who am I?
What am I?
Where am I?
Why am I?

Everywhere I turn,
the answer is not,
everywhere I looked,
the answer was not,
in despair,
I railed,
ranting,
I withdrew...

And there within,
to my wonder,
was the answer,
all along,
a light,
a beacon,
calling me,
pulling me,
ever onward,
ever closer,
toward home...

The answer once sought,

now remembered,
is the memory,
of Home...

Deep within,
the walls of my heart,
echo,
in the resonance,
of this song...

My heart sings,
with the joy,
of Home...

For once found,
the answer is,
that we are Home,
with God,
we are one,
In God...

For never,
were we parted,
and all that seems lost,
is yet a dream...

Awakening from the dream,
alive comes the world,
universes beyond count,

infinite wonders beheld,
in the heart of God...

I look in wonder,
and behold,
the splendor of all...

Wordless,
I cry,
like a child,
unable to grasp,
the ephemera,
in shock,
I weep,
at the beauty...

Of me...

For I see in me,
the essence,
the wonder,
of all,
of God...

Eons before me,
eons ahead,
time without limit,
the infinity,
of now,

of me,
of God...

In truth,
I reside,
resplendent,
its illumination,
the fire,
in God's eye...

We are the flame,
made of joy,
kindled,
in the heart of God,
our lives,
the magick,
the power of God,
set ablaze...

Here I remain,
in this resonance,
of remembrance,
my heart rekindled,
in blazing brilliance,
by the gentle hand,
of the Loving God...

Here I remain,
deep inside,

the beacon,
the guide,
I am the resonance,
calling...

I am calling you home,
I am calling remember,
and be whole...

For we are one,
You and I and God and We...

We are home,
and God has never left thee,
our names a thousand million be,
yet you may call me,
or name me you,
or name me Nephthys,
as you like,
a thousand names have I,
and even more beyond count,
or name me Amun,
but in our golden heart,
only one name matters...

You...

for your name,
has ever,

in all ways,
always been written,
deep within my heart,
my treasure,
my jewel,
hello You,
welcome home Me,
for we are one,
and You,
are all things,
to Me,
and I Love thee,
dear Golden Heart...

I Love thee,
and I call to thee,
hail,
and welcome home,
dear Me,
and together,
forever,
we all things Be...

By any other name,
I call thee,
and say to thee,
welcome home,
and remembered be...

14. Sobek: Love's Siren and Gentle Guide

Darkness surrounds,
the abyss enshrouds,
haunting echoes stir,
in this nightmare sea...

Lost in fear,
doubt abounds,
cast upon the sea of chaos,
we are lost,
dimly lit,
the void,
is endless,
utter despair,
its essence...

Without hope,
we perish,
still in sorrow,
we in fitful slumber,
dreaming dreams,
of drear and dread,
we surrender,
to the siren of terror...

Without hope,
we are lost,

in this nightmare,
of error...

Ever lost,
in this terror,
it seems forever,
a cacophonous error,
spun round,
dizzily held,
deep in this dread,
deep in the depths,
it seems we go,
to drown,
in sorrows shed,
we hanging,
by sanity's slimmest thread,
our purchase upon the cataract,
nearly dead...

Plunging now,
nearly dead,
in dread we fall,
falling,
forever lost,
till it seems,
the sea would have us,
engulf us,
in dread drown us,
and in dement,

erase us...

Till nothing is left,
and we are nothing more,
but the mad echoes,
that taunt the air...

Yet in that fractious second,
in that mad moment,
when all seems lost,
we are held,
not in the nightmare's,
noxious grip,
but by the hand,
of Love,
held gentle,
and dear,
all fear,
seems shear,
in this gentle presence...

At last we open,
our eyes,
and see,
before us,
light abounds,
so bright,
so beautiful,
to behold,

as we are held,
in the hand of Love...

All around,
gold shimmers,
the air,
filled with sweetness,
our hearts,
stutter,
in that first breath,
hope stirs,
alive,
another beat,
and we breathe,
the truth,
alive,
our beings filled,
with Love,
we thrive...

Around us we see,
each other alive,
and free...

Free from fear,
free to be,
free to see...

The sea before us,

is calm and clear,
as our hearts,
reflected,
we are...

In this heavenly space,
we feel,
the guiding hand,
of Love,
so free,
filling us,
with sight to see,
the depths,
the soul of we,
shining bright,
ever free,
at ease we rest,
and begin to see,
a pillar so bright,
a tower so light,
it shines...

The beacon,
of hope,
of Love,
beckons...

It calls,
it sings,

a song,
so sweet,
so clear,
singing,
a melody,
so dear,
our hearts are gladdened,
to hear...

Ever near we stray,
toward this tower,
enchanted,
entranced,
by its song,
so clear...

Until at last,
we chance,
upon its base,
and in stupendous awe,
we look,
up in wonder,
upon the face,
the face of the one held dear...

Into his eyes we stare,
in each eye,
universes born and die,
to be reborn again,

in his other eye...

In peace,
in ecstasy,
are we,
so happy,
we fly,
into his eyes,
the joining,
of him and I,
and we,
now his eyes,
seeing all,
being all,
for in his eyes,
all is Love,
all is hope,
and we are free...

We are free,
He I and We...

We are He,
we are the Tower,
we are the Pillar,
resting in our hearts,
calling to us,
reminding us,
we are free,

we are one,
we are thee...

Sobek,
the guide,
the pillar,
the tower,
the gentle hand,
of Love,
held dear,
in his eyes,
are we,
in his heart beheld,
are we,
in Love,
so clear...

In his eyes,
we behold,
the beauty,
the majesty,
of Amun,
in thee,
in his eyes,
we see,
that he and I and we,
are one,
in the heart of Amun,
and we are free...

15. After Life

Pure love,
awakens me,
gently suffused,
in joy,
I smile,
my eyes,
opened...

Below me,
before me,
the sea,
it's waves,
a soft,
sea green,
it's grasses,
undulating,
gently swaying,
swelling,

in its dancing way,
by breezes sweet play,
its soft caress,
Love's touch,
within my heart...

Above me,
the stars alight,
around them,
worlds abound,
each aglow,
in Love's light...

Reaching out,
I fly,
out among them,
Seeing,
in each,
infinities,
of worlds within,
landscapes contain,
tones jeweled,
pastel,
in colors silvered,
in lavender blue,
still others,
a golden,
ambered hue,
their skies,

alight,
in the flames,
of aragonite...

Turning,
slowly spinning,
worlds revolve,
I and them,
held,
within I Am,
by Love,
in its resolve,
the fount,
of creation,
everlasting...

Each world,
a sphere,
of ours,
and His making,
the dreams of our heart,
His fondest undertaking,
by purest heart,
our wishes granted,
the instant,
before our asking,
their landscapes,
the stuff of hope,
of magic,

our greatest imagining,
in joy,
made real,
the essence,
of life...

In life,
by Love,
is all,
interconnected,
by Love,
are we connected,
are we made,
each held,
in the heart,
of Love,
in the light,
of Love's power,
no boundary,
can stand,
in Love's presence,
no distance,
is found,
for His Love,
is all...

Returned,
I find myself,
looking within,

the starworlds,
have shone,
in the eyes of God,
as the spectrum,
a rainbowed hue,
now seeing...

After life,
is life still,
living,
unending,
everlasting,
the pattern,
now found,
is clear...

No distance,
no boundary,
in Love's light,
the worlds,
of matter,
of mind,
of spirit,
intertwine,
in Love's embrace,
as I am held,
in the arms of Love,
time ceases,
For I Am,

in peace,
in joy,
everlasting,
unending...

After life,
is life,
unending,
eternal,
we are,
death, lies dying,
for it is not,
and creation abounds,
on either side,
for the difference,
the distance,
is not...

Unending,
everlasting,
evermore,
we are...

16. Set Unbound

In Joy, Unbound:

 In the moment,
I surrender,
I am unbound,
unwound,
unwoven,
I unravel...

Floating free,
molecules dance,
spun round,
falling free,
I am,
in ecstasy...

Falling down,
into the ground,
I am,
part of all...

Deep down,
there is found,
within,
the deepest heart,
therein,

lost,
in the depths of love,
I am found...

In a million eyes,
I see,
above me,
the sky,
so free...

Spiraling upward,
I reach,
into the sky,
so free...

In joy,
I remember,
in love,
flying free...

In wonder,
I am,
the raven be...

Awed,
I hear,
the winds,
singing,
calling me...

Gliding,
higher and higher,
held aloft,
is my heart,
set free...

My heart,
so full,
so free,
it bursts to be...

Flying free,
swirling round,
in glorious,
exultant sound,
the stars are found,
dancing round...

Flying free,
Within the stars,
flying free,
among the stars,
in joy,
I am Set...

In the heart of all,
joy is found,
in the heart of all,

joy is unbound...

17. Hathor: The Heart of Love

Deep within the answer lies,
the heart of truth,
from sleep,
now stirs...

Beyond time,
she beckons,
calling softly,
singing sweetly,
of the song,
of Love...

In answer,
the heart awakens,
Love's light dawning,
within the sacred flame,
is kindled...

Love is a gentle healer,
before it,
pain is not,
sickness is gone,
separation is made whole,
communication is made clear,
like a river,
its waters cleansing,

breaking boundaries,
in its wake,
resolving all things,
restoring the soul,
by its power,
is the universe bound,
and made free,
from its essence,
the foundation,
the strength,
the formation,
of all...

All these things are She,
Goddess,
by whatever name,
be it Hathor,
or Ishtar,
or any other name besides,
but her name is Love,
and her name is yours,
for you are Loved,
and you are Love also...

All these things are yours,
Love's power is within you,
hear its call,
and awaken,
be free,

for You,
are Love's essence...

In whatever circumstance,
by whatever persuasion,
by whatever part of the rainbow,
you find yourself in,
be you male,
or be you female,
you are Love's essence...

18. Setekh Kheru

I

Against the dark abyss of night,
The wind stirs,
softly wailing,
Sifting sands,
In the distance,
The sound of thunder....

Upon the ground,
A boy sits,
Tending the flames,
Of his blazing fire,
Set against the chill of the night,
He stares deeply,
Into the flames,
Gently swaying,
He falls deeper,
Into dreams...

II

After a time,
He awakens,
With a start,
He sees a man walking,

Coming closer,
While in the distance,
The sound of thunder,
From all around,
Shaking the ground,
The sound of the storm,
Coming closer...

From deep in the night,
The man emerges,
The hem of his cloak,
Stirred by the breeze,
Sitting by the crackling blaze,
Laying his staff upon the sand,
He throws back his hood,
Revealing a shorn head,
Excepting the braid of hair,
Exclaiming his standing...

Greeting the boy,
Who sits by the blaze,
he gives him his name,
Saying,
"I am The Traveler,
And in thanks for your fire,
I shall tell you my tale..."

And so his story begins,
As all around them,

The wailing winds,
Begin to spin,
scattering the sands,
Lazily lifting them aloft,
On the breath of the wind...

III. The Tale of Two Brothers

In those ancient days,
Full of ancient ways,
There lived a pair of brothers,
Brothers so close,
They thought as one,
So close,
They spoke as one,
So close,
They felt as one...

In those hazy days,
In so many ways,
They would play,
In the great green nile,
Under that soft,
citrine sun,
They would dream,
Of the days to come,
Of the great deeds yet to be done...

Hazy days,

and dazey dreams,
Drifted by,
'Til the sun sat high in the sky,
A great amber eye,
Watching over them,
'Til they,
Watered by their dreams,
Could fly...

Grand dreams they dreamt,
Of vast plains,
Of starry skies and silver seas,
Of temples,
Of peoples,
Of lands unimagined...

Of such grand design,
Were these dreams,
So timeless,
So beautiful...

They could lose themselves...

The temple priests did warn them!...

And so it came to pass,
That in the plain of dreams,
That seed of doubt,
Did creep in...

It came to pass,
In the days,
When the sun,
So nearly set,
was a great carnelian blaze...

The priests did warn them,
To be wary,
To not lose focus,
And most of all,
To not lose hope...

The moment hope was lost,
The moment fear crept in,
That was the moment,
Their bond broke,
That was the moment,
They were set adrift,
Within the plain of dreams...

That was the moment of the serpent's birth...

Creature of chaos,
Creature of death,
Destroyer of worlds,
From his form,
Comes the void,
The black expanse,

The eternal emptiness...

In the moment of his birth,
All is darkness,
All is sadness,
All is death...

All that remains is despair...

The two brothers,
Lost in terror,
Aghast,
Adrift,
In the serpent's sea,
Must find each other,
Lest all souls,
Eternally damned be..

Within this endless void,
No time,
No space,
No place,
Could there be,
All is darkness eternally...

The two brothers,
Lost in this infinite sea,
Look they must within,
Deep inside they'll see,

Their hearts will ever be...

One to the other,
Their hearts call,
Asking them,
To remember,
Asking them,
To be...

In that moment,
They are found,
In that moment,
They are free,
In that moment,
The serpent ceases to be...

For they are the dreamers of dreams,
The builders of worlds,
The creators of infinity...

IV

Seeming as if from a dream,
The boy stirs in awe,
His mouth agape...

The traveler,
Having finished his tale,
Tells the boy,
"Ponder this well,
Discover the spell,
Awaken your heart,
Delve deep within,
And you'll never part,
For you were always one...

With me..."

V

In a flash of lightning,
And a rush of wind,
The raging storm,
Collapses,
And the sound,
Of roaring laughter,
Echoes on the night air...

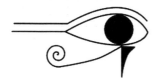

19. Amduat

I

Set in the night of jet,
Stars surround,
Sweetly swaying,
Softly humming,
Their song abounds,
As all around them,
Amun,
In his deepest dreaming,
Sings the song,
Of creation...

Sailing those starry seas,
The traveller,
To his wondrous delight,
Sees the stars alight,
In splendrous shades,
Of creamy jades,
Of the truest sapphire,

103

Of the clearest citrine,
Of the rarest ruby,
Of cheery calcite,
Of gossamer gold...

All of these,
His gaze beheld,
Reflected,
In the depths,
Of these obsidian seas...

II

Ever on these serene seas,
He sailed,
Ever on,
this great expanse,
He dreamed,
Of such worlds,
Of such wonders,
Other travelers,
He would tell,
Of tales,
Of worlds within worlds,
Of worlds of desire,
Of worlds of danger,
Of worlds of such beauty,
He wept,
His heart ached,

Lost in yearning,
He longed...

For so long,
He was lost,
Adrift,
Lost in memories,
Of better days,
Of things better said,
Of things better done,
Of the people,
He had left behind,
In lament,
He wept,
For the person,
He should've been...

So long ago,
He lost himself,
So long ago,
He forgot himself,
So long ago,
He set sail,
On this obsidian sea,
So long ago...

For so long,
He searched,
For so long,

He sought,
For so long,
He knew naught,
The way home...

Ever on...

III

Endless eternities reigned on,
'Til the serene sea,
Was not...

Now the sea,
Spinning slowly,
Spun round,
Faster and faster...

For once,
In this long eternity,
Hope dared to dawn...

Was this what he sought?...

The traveler knew of tales,
Both tall and true,
Speaking of the way,
Some say,
Of a whirlpool,

A great eye,
A passageway,
Set somewhere,
In this obsidian sea...

At last,
He had found it,
He found the passageway...

He had done it,
He was going home,
Deeper hope burned,
Deeper hope yearned,
In his deepest heart,
From darkest ember,
The light within burned,
A beacon,
Calling him home...

All around,
The starry sea,
Seemed to reflect,
To surround him,
In all its beauty,
In all its terror,
The life he once lived...

As he reached out,
As he touched the great eye,

He himself,
Became the mirror,
He himself,
Was the great eye...

At last he knew,
At last he remembered,
That he was always home,
That he always was,
Amun...

Appendix:

20: The Song Of Creation

I

Watching winds play,
Seeing the silver moon,
Hanging in the twilit sky,
In shades,
Indigo,
Amethyst,
And lavender blue...

A boy stands watching,
As the winds sway,
Dancing with the sand,
In a glorious way,
Winds that whirl,
Winds that spin,
High into the heavens,
Winds that signal,
A storm is coming,
The sound of thunder,
Night is on its way...

Standing,
Staring transfixed,

In awe,
At this magnificent sight,
The boy stands upon the precipice,
Of the temple,
Of the eternal night...

Amun Wehe...

They had come all this way,
On this sacred day,
To hear the great tale,
That is only told,
On this most sacred,
And holy day...

The day it was said,
That all things,
Upon the sand,
That all things,
Within the sky,
that all things,
Within the land,
Began...

II

"Meshru!... "

Upon hearing this,
The boy jolted,
Startled,
From his great reverie...

He ran from the entrance,
Deeper in,
Guided by the braziers,
Brightly lit,
Against the great chill,
on this great night...

The time of the telling,
Of the beginning,
Of it all...

Sitting now,
Amongst the others,
Gathered round,
In a circle,
Each now staring,
Excitedly waiting,
To hear the great tale...

As silence descended,

The only sound,
That of the wind,
As it whistled outside,
As it flickered the flames,
As their shadows,
Danced upon the wall,
Making the old language,
Come alive,
Making the old gods,
Dance and sway,
As between the shadows,
They did play...

Seeming to say,
Come with us,
Come and play,
Come with us,
And remember us,
In this way,
On this day...

It was in this way,
On this day,
That the boy's father,
The old man,
The wanderer,
The traveler,
The storyteller,
Began his story,

On this day,
And in his way...

III

Before all things,
There was darkness,
The void,
Chaos reigned,
The only thing there was,
Was Amun,
The infinite sea,
The great mystery...

From Amun,
Sprang all things,
He sang the gods,
He sang the seas,
He sang the land,
He sang the trees,
He sang the birds and bees,
He sang the dream,
Of you and me...

We sit upon this land,
The foundation,
The essence,
Of our bones,
Of our being,

Sift the sands,
Through your hands,
Hear his name,
Geb,
He is the land,
He is the sand
That danced into being,
As Amun sang...

Above him,
The sky came alive,
As he sang,
She came alive,
Nut,
The sky at night
The sky filled with stars,
Beautifully infinite,
Each star,
A brilliant eye,
The eyes of Amun,
As he guides our way,
Through the night,
And through the day...

In one eye,
Is held,
The brightness of the day,
Amun Re,
The eye,

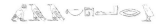

That guides us through our day...

The other,
Of silvered hue,
Guides us true,
In night's shade,
In dreams too,
His name is Khonsu,
The constant companion...

He sang then of the sea,
An infinite expanse,
Vast as He,
Filled with all manner of life,
Just as He,
And at night,
A mirror it be,
Between the sky and the sea,
A mirror she be,
Tefnut,
A mirror for He...

He sang of the winds,
An ocean of air,
Between the sky and the sea,
He sang the song,
He bade the breath of life,
To be,
His name is Shu,

He is the sound,
The vibration of creation...

The sea filtered by sand,
Became waters fresh and cool,
Flowing throughout the land,
Thus He sang,
Of rivers deep and wide,
Of waters flowing free,
Thus it was that Sobek came to be,
In his waters flowing free...

The time was ready,
The time was right,
The land was fertile,
The seas full of life,
The air was sweet,
Now was the time,
For the birth of man...

He dreamed him into being,
Breath, Body, and soul,
Wholly,
He gave of Himself,
Becoming man,
At the dawning of his being...

Thus was born man,
All around,

The new world,
Filled with such wonders,
Magical,
Terrible,
Delightful,
Through struggle,
Through bravery,
Man triumphed,
Through hope,
Through love,
Through strength,
Of heart,
Of soul,
Of mind,
Was magic given form,
In this new land,
In this new time,
In the dawning,
Of infinite possibility,
Was isis given form,
Deep within the heart of man...

In this new land,
In this new time,
Man explored,
Many things,
He discovered,
Strange lands,
He encountered,

With courage,
He surmounted all,
Thus from man's courage,
Was Horus born,
Though at times,
The struggle was hard,
The going was tough,
Still did man persevere,
Through sheer determination,
He succeeded,
His knowledge grew,
It was from that strength,
That determination,
That knowledge gained,
That Sekhmet grew,
A symbol of the will of Woman,
And man too...

Man's curiosity exponential,
His thirst for knowledge,
Boundless,
His blunders numerous,
His successes splendrous,
The only thing wanting,
The wisdom,
That lies between,
Outstretched mind,
And forgotten heart,
Find the balance,

And see the start,
Of ages countless,
Of peace and prosperity,
It is here you'll find me,
Thoth,
Wisdom is the key...

In the balance,
In the stillness,
Deep within,
Time is not,
Space is not,
Worlds abound,
Worlds of wonder,
Worlds of endless imagination,
Worlds of love,
Deep within,
The heart of all,
There I am,
Love,
There I am,
Hathor,
It is through love,
That worlds,
That children,
Are born,
It is in the hearts,
Of men and women,
That love is made,

And hope lives on...

Hopes,
Dreams,
Love,
These are the essence,
The life force of men,
Without which,
Life is not...

Throwing herbs into the braziers,
The teller of tales continued...

Dreams...

That is where life begins,
That is where life ends,
The place of dreams,
The duat,
The land of death,
The land of rebirth...

When the sun is done,
When night's shade,
Stirs upon the land,
When we dream,
Our final dream,
She comes,
Nephthys,

To guide us home,
To guide us,
To the halls of Maat,
Whence we shall be judged true,
Or if we be false,
The final end...

Maat,
The truth,
The balance,
Of deeds done,
Of thoughts good or fell,
Of words' spell,
The song of the soul,
Of gods and men...

The feather of Maat,
Floats above the scales,
Of life and death,
Be your heart filled,
With its light,
Live on you shall,
Else in darkness,
You shall dwell...

Your heart,
Your soul,
Deep within these,
He sees,

All that is true of you,
Your essence,
Laid bare,
By the eyes,
Of Anubis...

In essence,
Eternal,
In truth,
You remain,
Ever on,
Your journey continues,
Ever on,
Without end,
In the land of the dead,
You reign,
Osiris reborn,
Death is slain...

IV

Awakening from the dream,
Those gathered stir,
Only embers remain,
All around,
The shade of night,
Dark shadows abound,
The temple now darkened,
The traveler unfound,

Suddenly laughter,
An ominous sound
Spinning round,
Taunting those gathered,
'Til none are found,
To the winds all scattered,
As on the wall,
Before there was naught,
Now stands a figure,
Of a jeering jackal...

Made in the
USA
Columbia, SC